HANNIBAL:
MARK TWAIN'S BOYHOOD HOME

Linda R. Wade

ROURKE ENTERPRISES, INC.
Vero Beach, FL 32964

Library of Congress Cataloging-in-Publication Data

Wade, Linda R.
    Hannibal: Mark Twain's boyhood home / by Linda R. Wade.
    p. cm. — (Doors to America's past)

    Includes index.
    Summary: Describes the history and development of Hannibal, Missouri, and the life of one of its most famous citizens, the author Mark Twain.
    ISBN 0-86592-466-X
    1. Twain, Mark, 1835-1910 – Biography – Youth – Juvenile literature. 2. Twain, Mark, 1835-1910 – Homes and haunts – Missouri – Hannibal – Juvenile literature. 3. Authors, American – 19th century – Biography – Juvenile literature. 4. Literary landmarks – Missouri – Hannibal – Juvenile literature. 5. Hannibal (Mo.) – History – Juvenile literature. [1. Twain, Mark, 1853-1910. 2. Authors, American. 3. Hannibal (Mo.) – History.] I. Title. II. Series: Wade, Linda R. Doors to America's past.
PS1332.W28 1991
818'.409 – dc20
[B]
[92]   90-8980
                                                                 CIP
                                                                 AC

Acknowledgments

    Special thanks to Henry Sweets, Curator of the Mark Twain Museum; Dorothy Miniar, Director of the Hannibal Visitor's and Convention Bureau; and Robert C. Bogart, J. Hurley and Roberta Hagood, George Wallery, and the many other people who supplied information, assistance, and pictures.

Photo Credits

Hannibal Free Public Library: 8
El Dorado County Historical Society - Placerville, California: 13
Mark Twain Papers, The Bancroft Library - University of California, Berkeley: 4, 35
Becky Thatcher Book Shop: cover, 7, 19, 22, 24, 26, 28, 30, 37, 39, 41, 43, 45
Mark Twain's Boyhood Home: 47
Mark Twain Cave: 44

Table of Contents

Introduction

Mark Twain as a child

Hannibal is a quiet Missouri town with a population of only about 20,000, but it has a special history. It is the town where one of America's most famous writers grew up.

Samuel Langhorne Clemens, known to everyone as Mark Twain, lived in this little Mississippi River town from the age of 4 to 17. He roamed the hills around Hannibal, he climbed the trees, he explored the caves, he had a special friend with whom he shared endless adventures, he knew a pretty girl who stole his heart. He painted fences. When he grew up, he wrote about these childhood experiences in books such as *The Adventures of Tom Sawyer* and *The Adventures of Huckleberry Finn.*

The characters in these books—Tom, Huck, Becky Thatcher, Aunt Polly, and Injun Joe, to name but a few—are all based on people Mark Twain knew during his childhood in Hannibal. Twain's books became so popular that each year many people began to visit the little town. In that way, his characters have continued to "live" there.

It is now more than 150 years since young Sam Clemens was growing up in Hannibal, but visitors still come to see the home of their beloved author. They still come to dream and to watch the mighty Mississippi from Cardiff Hill. Tom Sawyer's fence still gets a good whitewashing every now and again. And visitors still roam the cave that young Sam once explored, and where Tom and Becky were lost. Hannibal is still Mark Twain country. Hannibal will always be Mark Twain country.

1
The Beginnings of Hannibal

When a government surveying party worked its way through the Missouri Territory in 1818, it found a perfect valley for a settlement. Located on the Mississippi River 120 miles north of St. Louis, this fine wooded piece of land was nestled between two limestone bluffs. A stream, later named Bear Creek, weaved through the middle of the valley. The bluff that later would be called Holliday's Hill created the natural northern boundary. It was to become Cardiff Hill in Mark Twain's writings.

The southern border of the valley was formed by the bluff later known as Lover's Leap. It got its name from Native American lore and pioneer stories of star-crossed lovers who came to tragic ends there.

When the weather grew cold, the surveying team built a cabin on this pleasant land and, before returning home, spent the winter there. That was the beginning of Hannibal.

The next year, another surveying party headed back north from St. Louis. This time the team had a special mission. It was to find land for people who had become

Lover's Leap

homeless in a severe earthquake that had occurred several years before in New Madrid, a town in southern Missouri. This surveying team also found the green and pleasant spot between the bluffs, the perfect place for a settlement. Their mission was accomplished.

The actual settlement of the new area, however, was a slow process. One reason was that people feared confrontations with the Native Americans who lived there and who did not welcome white people's encroachments on

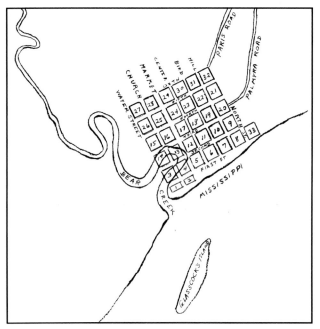

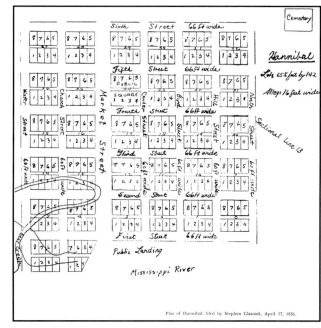

First plat of Hannibal, 1819

Plat of Hannibal, 1836

their land. When stories spread of problems with the natives, people hesitated to buy land there.

Another reason for Hannibal's slow growth was that there were some overlapping claims to the territory. Until clear titles to the land could be established, sale of land stopped. And lastly, getting to Hannibal suddenly became a problem. A sand bar had developed at the mouth of Bear Creek where it emptied into the Mississippi. The sand bar kept boats from landing at Hannibal or going upstream.

By 1830, there were only 30 people living in the tiny town.

2
Hannibal Grows

In spite of a slow start, Hannibal was destined to grow. As settlers moved West, the town's population expanded.

In the mid-1830s, businessmen from New York and Boston sold land to a number of Easterners who were eager to move West. The land was in a place called Marion City, not far from Hannibal. People came by the boatload and started building houses. But Marion City was on low land and, in 1836, was washed out by a flood. Still, the residents liked the new territory and wanted to relocate somewhere nearby. As it turned out, by then Hannibal had its land titles cleared and was ready to receive settlers. People from Marion City flocked to Hannibal—even though they had, not too long before, considered themselves superior to Hannibal. In the spirit of frontier competitiveness, the people of Marion City at one time had referred to Hannibal as a "frog pond" and "graveyard." But unlike Marion City, Hannibal rises up and away from the Mississippi, and flooding was not a severe problem there. The washed-out citizens of Marion

City suddenly were quite happy to settle in this "inferior"—but high and dry—"frog pond"!

Not long after that, Mother Nature also stepped in once again to help Hannibal's growth. High water from the spring thaws inland washed a lot of brush down Bear Creek and piled it against the sand bar at the mouth of the stream. When the Mississippi rose, the channel was blocked so the river's mighty waters washed the brush and the sand bar away. Hannibal, now easy to get to, began to attract increasing numbers of settlers. By the time Sam Clemens and his family arrived in Hannibal in 1839, there were about 700 people living there. When Sam left 14 years later, the population had grown to 4,000.

3

Life on the River

During the time that the Clemens family lived in Hannibal, the town was growing into a busy agricultural and business center. The Mississippi River was becoming America's highway, with barges and boats daily plying its waters and transporting many kinds of cargo up and down its course. Hannibal became an important stop. There, grain, tobacco and various other agricultural products from the surrounding area were loaded onto barges for shipment as far north as Wisconsin and as far south as New Orleans. Steamboats, too, were coming into the peak of their popularity and stopped regularly in Hannibal. With their steady passenger list of businessmen, fur traders, pioneers, peddlers, missionaries, and every other imaginable sort of traveler, steamboats stirred up a lot of activity each time they arrived in the little town.

Meat-packing became a big industry in this busy town that was so conveniently located on the big river. An 1849 newspaper article reported that 1,500 head of cattle and 13,500 hogs were slaughtered in Hannibal for shipment to St. Louis. But if the meat-packing business was a prosperous one, it also created quite a commotion in

Hannibal. Imagine hogs and cattle—squealing, snorting, and dashing about—as they were herded through the streets of the town. That was the only way to get the animals from the backcountry, where they were raised, to the packing plants along the riverbank. And the streets in rugged frontier towns such as Hannibal were made simply of dirt. Imagine the dust and mud—and even more pandemonium along the way as horses, tied to posts in town, were startled by the tumult and added their own protests to the scene.

Understandably, such disturbances interfered with other business in the town and created problems for downtown merchants. But they rarely complained. The sale of livestock and the meat-packing business meant cash for the farmers and packinghouse workers. That meant increased sales for the merchants. As the town grew, however, the livestock herding routes were moved to the outskirts of Hannibal, sparing the growing town center a lot of wild activity.

In 1859, a rail connection to St. Joseph, in the westernmost part of Missouri, provided a direct link across the state for people moving to the new frontiers. St. Joseph also was the eastern end of the Pony Express, the great communication link to the West, and it was the

Pony Express

starting point of several big wagon trains going west. With a direct link to a city as important as St. Joseph, Hannibal's position as a trading center grew. With the introduction of the railroad to America, river traffic had declined somewhat, but Hannibal was fortunate enough to get the railroad. It then had both the river and the railroad.

4
War and Peace

By 1860, the time of the Civil War, Hannibal was one of the leading communities in the thriving state of Missouri, but the town's peace and prosperity would soon come to an abrupt halt. With the coming of the war, the state suddenly found itself in an odd criss-crossing of allegiances. Missouri had been admitted into the Union as a slave state, but it voted to stay in the Union during the war. And as it turned out, a large part of northern Missouri, originally settled by people from the South, supported the South. At the same time, a large part of southern Missouri, originally settled by people from the North, supported the North. Hannibal, being in northern Missouri, officially supported the South even though there were many free-spirited people in the town who disagreed and supported the Northern cause.

If it sounds confusing, that's because it was! There were political differences even in the Clemens family. Sam's brother Orion was a passionate supporter of the North. In the meantime, Sam decided to support the South though it was not great political conviction that caused him to enlist in the Confederate Army. He did so largely just to defend his little corner of Missouri from invasion—and even his mild support for the Confederacy did not last long. After only two weeks, he left the Confederate volunteers and joined his brother to go west. There Orion would serve a federal appointment in the new Nevada territory, and Sam would try his hand at prospecting and newspaper reporting.

In Hannibal, meanwhile, Union troops occupied the town for most of the war, and many conflicts of allegiance continued to divide neighbors and families. It was a disturbing time. Business slowed almost to a standstill as people feared to move about freely.

After the war, Hannibal turned to the production of manufactured goods, but it was not an easy time for the town. Its business life was all but gone from years of inactivity, and transportation systems on the river had all but died when the river was closed to commerce during the war. Nonetheless, Hannibal took its first plunge into trade, and lumber became the town's first important product. Lumber mills sprang up along Bear Creek, with logs for the sawmills being floated down the Mississippi from Minnesota and Wisconsin. That was easier and more economical than building a railroad north to the forests. Hannibal's location on the river once again contributed to the town's prosperity. The lumber business boomed. And with one railway going west to St. Joseph and another pushing south to St. Louis, Hannibal developed an even wider market for lumber in the nation's reviving economy after the war.

In 1872, one of the first railway bridges across the Mississippi was constructed at Hannibal. The bridge gave the town rail connections to Chicago, a big commercial center at the time. The important rail connection contributed to Hannibal's business growth, and the town then added railcar roundhouses, repair shops, and switching yards to its landscape.

Toward the end of the century, shoe manufacturing became a big part of Hannibal's economy. Hundreds of thousands of shoes were made there before the business slowed down and finally closed in the 1960s.

5
Hannibal Today

Hannibal now manufactures a variety of products. Boats, lawnmowers, and tool and die equipment are produced, and some meat industry still exists in Hannibal—though in a somewhat more quiet version than the 1840s livestock drives through the town center! In the 1960s, one Hannibal company produced all of the deviled ham west of the Mississippi, and the company is still in business, having expanded its operation to include other canned food products.

The river still offers many shipping opportunities. It is still used to transport grain and other agricultural products; and the smaller specialty manufacturing companies also have found Hannibal's river location convenient for moving their products easily. In fact, the whole area around Hannibal is still generously supported by the great river. Fertilizers and chemical products are produced just north of Hannibal and are quickly shipped out by way of the river. In Ilasco, a small town south of Hannibal, limestone is mined and cement made. Ilasco's old cement plant had a special place in history: it made most of the cement that was used in building the Panama

Canal. Ocean-going barges carried the cement down the river to Panama.

In 1900, Hannibal had a population of about 20,000, and it remains about the same today, but Hannibal's city limits have expanded greatly. When young Sam Clemens lived in Hannibal, the town extended only six blocks from the river. Today, you can drive five miles and still be in Hannibal. Much of the newer area, too, contains striking bluffs and wooded hills. When morning mists and fogs lying in the river valley slowly curl and rise to the sky, the town can take on a uniquely mysterious and tranquil beauty. Such magical and mysterious mists must have fascinated the imaginative young Sam on his morning rounds of favorite places.

Hannibal's weather varies with the seasons. Summer days are sunny, hot, and from the closeness of the river, often humid. They're the lazy summer days you read about in Mark Twain's books. Winter means cold. You can picture Sam and his friends skating on the Mississippi's vast frozen expanse or imagine pieces of Mississippi ice being collected and stored to keep food cool in the warmer months to come. Today, the river no longer freezes over. Its level and temperature have been raised by a system of dams, falls, and floodways. But

Mark Twain

you'll still feel the same crisp nip of freezing air that hurried Sam to his wintertime adventures.

At first glance, Hannibal appears to be like any other small town on the Mississippi. But soon the visitor senses a unique charm and special mood about the place that Mark Twain called St. Petersburg in his books. St. Petersburg is Hannibal. It was Mark Twain's boyhood home.

6
Sam Clemens, Mark Twain

Mark Twain gave life to many characters in his books, but he is closest to Tom Sawyer. In fact, the character of Tom Sawyer is a combination of Twain as a young boy and several of Twain's young friends. But so vivid is Twain's writing that it's hard to think of Tom as a fictional character. And, indeed, as a young boy growing up on the Mississippi River, Twain had countless adventures just like the ones he wrote about in his books. Who was this talented man who recreated, for generations of readers, the thrills and perils and adventures and unique joys of childhood?

Mark Twain, born Samuel Langhorne Clemens, came into the world on November 30, 1835 in tiny Florida, Missouri. It was a doubly festive day: as Sam appeared in the world, Halley's Comet appeared in the sky. Perhaps it was an especially promising sign, for the infant Sam would need a lot of help. Born weak and sickly, he wouldn't outgrow his frail health and puniness until the age of seven, when he at last became a robust and rugged boy.

When Sam was four years old, his family moved to Hannibal, where his father ran a general store and later became a judge. Sam had one sister and three brothers. Two other children died young. His mother had great patience with Sam, for not only was he sickly as a child, but he was also full of mischief. To help his health, Mrs. Clemens gave Sam an endless round of tonics, home remedies, and popular medicines even long after he out-grew his need for them. To tame his over-active charac-ter, she tried any number of methods and persuasions, but they seldom had the desired effect on the indepen-dent Sam.

Sam's relationship with his father was never close. The dignified but stern Judge Clemens could never quite understand his unpredictable, imaginative, and sensitive son. And the red-haired, curly-headed Sam, though full of pranks and playfulness, also was a sensitive child. But Sam was very close to his mother. It was from the fun-loving, good-humored, and warm-hearted Mrs. Clem-ens that Sam acquired so much of his impulsiveness and independence. And a determined soul he was from the start, in spite of his innocent-looking face. He knew what he liked and what he didn't like. Once, when an epidemic of sickness broke out in Hannibal, Mrs. Clemens set out

Mark Twain Home and Memorial Fence

two bottles of medicine, one for Sam and one for his brother Henry. Sam didn't like the medicine at all, so every day he measured out his teaspoonful and poured it into the cracks in the floor. He later commented that the results had, after all, proved quite successful. "The epidemic never broke out under our house!" he pointed out.

7

Sam, Steamboats, and the Mississippi

For young Sam, one of the most exciting events of the day was a steamboat's docking in Hannibal. A great deal of Hannibal's life was shaped by its being located on the Mississippi. And the influence of the river and river life was no less important for Sam—as a young boy, later as a river pilot, and throughout his life.

It never failed to thrill him: someone would call out, "S-t-e-a-m-boat a-comin'!" and the whole town surged to life. Businessmen left their shops, children left their games, housewives left their chores, men passing leisure time left their checkerboards. The steamboat was bringing the outside world to Hannibal. There would be mail to be delivered and a whole assortment of new merchandise from peddlers and visitors coming to town. Later, outgoing packages would be checked for loading, and passengers would say their final good-byes before boarding the boat.

There were things to watch for even before the boat docked. As a steamboat neared the landing, all the children strained their eyes to catch sight of the symbol on

Steamboat at levee

the boat. Each boat had a different one—an anchor, a bale of cotton, or an animal head. It was an honor to be the first to recognize and announce the boat's symbol.

Docking the boat, in itself, was a thrilling event. Deck hands would expertly throw a rope around a post on shore and then skillfully tighten it with a special knot. Sam never missed a move. He watched carefully as the passengers and crew disembarked while others boarded. There was so much to see as people were continually bumping and jostling each other. From what far-off places did these people come? Some men wore elegant, tall stovepipe hats, others wore bandannas. Some women wore elaborate hoop skirts, others were in faded cotton wraps. And in only 10 spellbinding minutes, all of the unloading and loading and disembarking and boarding had to be completed, for then the Captain would promptly announce that the boat was leaving.

Sam would watch as the boat, fired by its mighty engines, started moving, the water behind it churning into a heavy foam. And he'd gaze at the smoke billowing out of the smokestacks of the departing vessel. Only when all traces of the boat were gone did he ever leave the dock. The next steamboat would never come too soon for Sam. "Someday," he said, "I'm going to be a steamboat captain." It was a dream that would come true in later years.

When Sam had a choice of going to school or being near the river, the river often won out. Sometimes he and some of his friends would play "hooky" and spend the day on Glasscock's Island near the Illinois side of the river. In *Tom Sawyer*, the island became Jackson's Island. On one such river adventure, the boys took someone's little boat and rowed over to the island. There they found turtle eggs, which they cooked, and they explored the island, playing Robinson Crusoe. Time slipped by, and before the

Tom and Huck on raft

boys knew it, the sun was beginning to set. They headed
home as quickly as they could but Sam knew he'd never
make it on time. To avoid waking his mother and getting
the thrashing he knew would surely be his, Sam decided
to delay the punishment by stopping at his father's office.
His father had long since left the building, so Sam
climbed in through a little window. When he got in and

looked down, he saw the still, gray face of a stranger lying on the floor. The man's eyes were open but looked strangely like a pair of bulging marbles. It was a corpse Sam was looking at! Unbeknownst to him, someone had murdered the man, and the body had been put into Judge Clemens' office to await the next day's court hearing. The scene was one that Sam would not soon forget. He wrote about it later, but by then, he added his usual good humor: "I went away from there. I do not say that I went away in any sort of hurry. . . . I went out the window, and I carried the sash [window frame] along with me; I did not need the sash, but it was handier to take it than to leave it. . . ."

When Sam was nine years old, he had his first steamboat ride—an overnight trip to St. Louis. He was so excited that for days before he bragged to his friends. When the day finally arrived, he could all but contain his excitement as his father showed him around the boat and even allowed him to stay up much later than usual to listen to the travelers' stories. His excitement was all the more stirred up by reports that one group of passengers made about a terrible steamboat fire that had just occurred in New Orleans. It turned out to be more excitement than even the brave and fearless Sam had wished for. After he

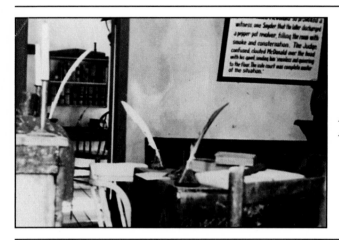

*Law office of Judge Clemens,
Mark Twain's father*

went to sleep, he must have started dreaming. (In fact, all of his life Sam had unusually vivid and often frightening dreams. Coupling this with a habit of sleepwalking, he gave his family many a nighttime scare.)

But Sam suddenly awakened from his dream, sure he saw a flame through the boat's window. He jumped from his bed and dashed about yelling, "Fire! Fire!" Most of the people ignored him, undoubtedly thinking that he was just having a bad dream. Sam was so embarrassed that the next morning, with head bowed, he left the boat as quietly as possible. But his first steamboat venture, however startling, did nothing to dampen his love for boats or the river.

8
Young Sam's Friends

Sam—fun-loving, rugged, generous-hearted, and a natural leader—had many friends. One of his best was Tom Blankenship. Tom's parents didn't make him go to school, so he lived as he pleased. Most boys envied him. Mrs. Clemens, fearing a bad influence on Sam, tried to keep the boys apart, but they had codes and often met at night. To get Sam's attention, Tom would meow like a cat or whistle like a bird. Sam would wait until his brother was asleep; then he'd crawl out his bedroom window, and the two boys would be off on their daring escapades.

In Tom, Sam had the perfect partner for adventure. The two boys fished in the Mississippi and swam in Bear Creek; they dug for treasure, explored miles of caves, tramped through the woods, and roamed around cemeteries. Tom became Huckleberry Finn in Mark Twain's books.

Another special friend was Anna Laurie Hawkins. Her family moved to Hannibal when Sam was six years old. In time she would capture the heart of young Sam Clemens. They walked to and from school together, and Sam often

Tom Sawyer's room

carried her books. Once, when a spelling bee was down to only Laura and Sam, he misspelled a word on purpose so that Laura could win. She later became Becky Thatcher in his books.

Though Sam might occasionally be a finalist in a school spelling bee, he was never an eager student. He preferred learning from his boyish exploits, not from books, but that would not always be the case. When he was 13, one day he was walking along and the wind blew a piece of paper to his feet. It was a page from a book about Joan of Arc, the young French girl who died while defending her country from England. Sam stood stunned and speechless over the exciting words he read on the page. It was a turning point in his life. In that moment, he developed a deep desire to read and learn, especially about history. He became an intense and avid reader, a love that remained with him for the rest of his life.

Some of Sam's other childhood friends included cousins who lived on a farm about 40 miles from Hannibal. Even as an adult, Twain recalled that the "golden summers" he spent on the farm of his good-hearted Uncle John Quarles were among the happiest times of his youth. There was never enough time to explore the endless adventures that were possible in such a glorious country setting. And it came complete with a huge and wonderful flock of ever-ready playmates—his eight young cousins as well as the children of his uncle's slaves. Having been born into a slaveholding society, Sam was familiar with slavery. At one time his father kept a household slave, though the Missouri slave system was not as rigid as the one in the plantation economy of the deep South. Sam, who came to view slavery as a "peculiar institution," always had a special sense of companionship with the

Black people he knew when he was growing up. If there never was enough time for play on his uncle's farm, neither was there enough time to listen to the slaves tell all of their fearsome tales of mystery, night terrors, ghosts, evil spirits, and danger that was ready and waiting to pounce at every corner. These Black storytellers could not be matched in the art of creating vivid and thrilling tales of suspense. It was from them that Twain first learned to imagine the kind of tales of sheer terror that later would enliven some of his books.

9

Sam Goes to Work

When Sam was 12 years old, tragedy struck the Clemens household. Judge Clemens fell ill with pneumonia and died. Sam had to go to work after school to help make ends meet at home. His father, though ambitious and hard-working, had always struggled to make a living. He left his family no money. Sam went to work for a printer and before long became the printer's apprentice. He learned the business so well that he later was able to help his brother Orion in the newspaper business. Working for a newspaper also was the beginning of his writing career. When his brother was away—or wasn't looking—Sam would sometimes slip a humorous item into the paper. At times the ever-playful Sam went overboard with his writing pranks and got himself into trouble. But he also realized that he enjoyed storytelling and that he liked the reactions he got as a writer. He started writing articles and submitting them to magazines and newspapers for publication.

When he was 18, Sam left Hannibal and became a printer in St. Louis and later in New York and

Philadelphia. Sam, who had a life-long love of travel, never had qualms about venturing to new places.

But however far he roamed from his beloved river, Sam never lost his desire to become a riverboat captain. When the opportunity came for him to work on a steamboat, he left the printing business. His happiness at finding work that he truly loved, however, was mixed with great sadness. Tragedy struck again when his brother Henry was killed in a riverboat explosion. Sam always felt responsible because he had encouraged his brother to work on a steamboat.

Sam was 23 when he became an apprentice riverboat pilot. He studied intensely, memorizing thousands of details by heart and learning every bend, turn, curve, channel, and bank formation of the Mississippi River from St. Louis all the way down to New Orleans. And he had to know the river not just by day, but by night, too. Securing his license 18 months later was one of the proudest moments of his life, and he became known as one of the best pilots on the river.

The name he used as a writer came from those piloting days. When a crew member wanted to signify that the water ahead was safe, he would call out a riverboat term,

Twain as riverboat captain

"ma-a-ark twa-ain." Apparently Sam liked the sound of the call and he took it for his pen name—the fictitious name that authors sometimes use for their writing.

However great Sam's love for his river piloting, the work didn't last long. Not even two years after he got his license, the Civil War put an end to his career by closing the Mississippi to commercial traffic. But Sam always treasured the memories of his time on the river. He later wrote *Life on the Mississippi*, in which he vividly describes his beloved river piloting days.

With the coming of war, neither did Sam's military career last very long. After being a Confederate volunteer for only two weeks, he left the service and headed west with his brother Orion. There Sam first worked as a gold prospector. He didn't find any gold, but he did meet many interesting people. He later wrote a humorous book, *Roughing It*, which told of his prospecting days. And he helped make California's Calaveras County famous with stories such as "The Jumping Frog of Calaveras County," published after his stay there.

It was while Sam was a newspaper reporter later in Nevada that he first used his pen name, Mark Twain. He went on to write many books and articles under the name. All of his books were published between 1869 and 1897. Two of his most famous—and the ones that make Hannibal come fully alive—are *The Adventures of Tom Sawyer*, published in 1876, and *The Adventures of Huckleberry Finn*, published in 1885. Two of his other well-known books are *A Connecticut Yankee in King Arthur's Court* and *The Prince and the Pauper*.

Mark Twain's middle and later years were as full and active as his early ones. He married at the age of 35 and had four children. His writing made him prosperous and famous, but, as in his earlier years, tragedy was a frequent companion. His son died as an infant, and two of his daughters died as young adults. In addition, at one point he had to declare bankruptcy because of the failure of a publishing company he owned. But he also lived well

Mark Twain as a white-haired adult

and happily for 20 years in Hartford, Connecticut, where he wrote most of his best books. He and his family traveled widely and lived in Europe for several years. Between writing projects, he lectured extensively. He was always a wonderfully funny man, so his down-to-earth stories and humorous style made him a very popular speaker. The boy from Hannibal became one of the world's most celebrated personalities.

Twain returned to Hannibal as often as he could. His last visit was in 1902 while enroute to Columbia, Missouri, to receive an honorary degree from the University of Missouri.

Samuel Clemens died on April 21, 1910, as Halley's Comet blazed across the sky. It had also blazed through the sky on the day he was born 75 years earlier. In Sam's case, the comet surely flashed a fiery streak first as an announcement of—and then as a salute to—a very special man.

10

A Visit to Hannibal

There are many things to see in this pleasant little Mississippi River town. Hannibal is, above all, Mark Twain country. To boys and girls, it is the capital of youth and youthful adventure. To adults, it's a place to recapture a sense of their own bygone childhood.

One place a visitor surely wants to see at the first opportunity is Mark Twain's Boyhood Home and Museum, built by his father, Judge Clemens. Sam lived in the house from 1844 to 1853. Many of Sam's adventures started from this house, and many of the friends he had while living here later became characters in his books. You can go through the dining room, kitchen, parlor, and his bedroom. Is that Sam you see sneaking out the window for a secret meeting with his friend Tom?

In 1911, the house was scheduled to be torn down in a city renovation project, but a local attorney, George Mahan, recognized its importance and bought the house. After restoring it, he gave it to the city of Hannibal.

Tom Sawyer's fence is next to the house. In *Tom Sawyer*, Aunt Polly tries to get Tom to paint the fence, but he

Twain house dining room and parlor

Whitewashing the fence

gets out of it by telling his friends what an honor it is to paint the fence. He manages to get them not only to do the job, but to pay him for the privilege of doing so!

In 1935, when Hannibal was celebrating Mark Twain's 100th birthday, a museum was established next to the house. The ivy-covered, gray stone building contains a number of Twain's personal items, including one of the famous white coats that he so often wore as an adult, a Mississippi river pilot's wheel, and the desk at which he wrote *Tom Sawyer*. The museum also houses 16 paintings by the famous American artist, Norman Rockwell, who liked to paint scenes from the *Tom Sawyer* stories. The museum shop is a good place to buy Twain mementos.

Across the street is the Becky Thatcher Bookshop. It was the home of Laura Hawkins, the girl who stole young Sam's heart and on whom Twain based his character of Becky Thatcher. On the ground floor you can buy just about every book ever written by or about Mark Twain. Upstairs are the restored parlor and bedroom, much as they looked when Sam and Laura were schoolmates.

A "mere frog's leap away," as Twain would say, is the Clemens Law Office, where Sam's father presided as

Mark Twain Museum and Boyhood Home

Becky Thatcher's House

Justice of the Peace and where Sam found the terrifying corpse. From there, walk over to Cardiff Hill, one of Sam's favorite playgrounds. At the foot of the hill you'll see a bronze statue of Tom Sawyer and Huckleberry Finn, ready to go "fishin'." Sam and Tom spent many a day fishing on the Mississippi.

Now take a deep breath and start climbing the many steps up Cardiff Hill. You'll probably be as out of breath as Sam must've been the many times he went up those heights. On the other hand, he had a lot of practice, so maybe the climb was a snap for him! When you get to the top of the hill, you'll see a white lighthouse, a fine old beacon for river traffic. And you'll get a wonderful view of Hannibal and many miles of the Mississippi River.

Probably one of the most exciting—and most popular—places to visit in Hannibal is the Mark Twain Cave. In *Tom Sawyer*, Twain called it McDougal's Cave. That's where Tom and Becky use up their last match without finding the cave entrance and then are lost in the cave's stark and terrifying blackness. You can recapture some of the sheer drama of their adventure with the help of a special tour available at the cave.

The Tom Sawyer Dioramas Museum features miniature scenes, called dioramas, that tell the story of Tom

Tom Sawyer and Huck Finn statue

Lighthouse on Cardiff Hill

Sawyer. These scenes, with hand carved figures presented in remarkable detail, are complete, down to the "spilt" jam in Aunt Polly's pantry. The story of each scene is on a tape you can listen to as you walk along.

Most of the places you'll want to see in Hannibal are within walking distance of each other, but you might want to hop a train or a buggy for a narrated tour through the whole town. There's the Twainland Passenger Express and a horse-drawn buggy called the Mark Twain Clopper. A city tour will give you a rounded-out sense of

43

Mark Twain Cave entrance

the place that gave birth to so many of Twain's characters. If you're free in the middle of the day, a wonderful way to relax is to take a one-hour riverboat cruise. It includes a commentary on river history and legend and floats you down the wide Mississippi past Jackson's Island and Lover's Leap. The cruise then turns and goes up the river past Cardiff Hill as well as huge grain silos built in more modern times. In Sam's day, grain was stored in sacks and barrels before being loaded onto barges. Today, grain is pumped quickly out of the silos into the shipping vessels. As the tour boat's pilot blows the whistle, you can sense the excitement that Sam always felt as a boy waiting for the riverboats to dock.

Mississippi River steamboat and bridge

National Tom Sawyer Days are held in Hannibal each year on the first weekend in July. The National Fence Painting Contest recalls Tom Sawyer's scheme to get Aunt Polly's fence painted without doing the work himself. Then there's the Frog Jump-Off in which children get to jump a frog. The longest jump wins a prize. Another contest selects a Tom Sawyer and Becky Thatcher from a local school to represent Twain's characters at official events. The four Tom Sawyer Days are filled with loads of fun—entertainment, history, food, crafts, and fireworks.

Another festive time in Hannibal is the two-day Historic Folklore Festival held in late October or early November. That's when the past comes alive with costumes, homemade pies and cakes, and handcrafts. Crafts-workers demonstrate their skills in oldtime crafts, and there's lots of music.

Hannibal truly belongs to Mark Twain, and you'll see his "presence" everywhere. In addition to all of the official places and buildings that commemorate the author, there are Twain remembrances popping up in a few unexpected places, too. If you're hungry, you can get a sandwich called the Mark Twain Burger, and if you like chicken, you can choose from an Aunt Polly, a Huck Finn, or a Tom Sawyer Chicken Box. There are motels and other lodgings whose names herald the life and characters of the famous former resident, and galleries, shops, streets, and even a lake call forth his memory, too.

In the next few years, more Twain commemorative buildings will be added to the existing ones. There are plans for a print shop like the one where Sam learned the printing trade as a young boy, and a one-room school-house is being built to resemble the one Sam attended. In it, visiting children will learn more about Mark Twain, his writings, and his life in the river town.

A visit to Hannibal is a visit into the life and mind of a great American writer. Mark Twain largely identified

Mark Twain standing in doorway during his last visit to Hannibal in 1902

himself with only one town—Hannibal—and that town keeps his memory alive for the many people who are still drawn to the wonderful worlds that he created in his books. So great is Twain's presence in the town that a visitor almost expects to spot the older white-haired Twain just about anytime, stepping through a doorway as he, too, comes back to visit his childhood town. Perhaps his popularity is so great because he helps us to recall and relive our own childhood memories. There's a little bit of Tom Sawyer and Becky Thatcher in all of us, and Hannibal is there to help us find it.

Index